delicious diabetic recipes

P9-CQV-610

Easy Everyday Lunches

easy everyday lunches

Main-Dish Chicken Soup

   6 cups fat-free reduced-sodium chicken broth
   1 cup grated carrots
   ½ cup diced red bell pepper
   ½ cup frozen green peas
   ½ cup sliced green onions
   1 seedless cucumber
  12 chicken tenders (about 1 pound), halved
   ½ teaspoon white pepper

1. Bring broth to a boil in large saucepan or Dutch oven over high heat. Add carrots, bell pepper, peas and green onions; return to a boil. Reduce heat; simmer 3 minutes.

2. Meanwhile, cut ends off cucumber and discard. Using vegetable peeler, start at top and make long, noodle-like strips of cucumber. Cut any remaining cucumber pieces into thin slices. Add cucumber to saucepan; cook 2 minutes over low heat.

3. Add chicken tenders and white pepper; simmer 5 minutes or until chicken is cooked through.   *Makes 6 servings*

Serving Suggestion: Serve with a small mixed green salad and French bread.

Nutrients per Serving: 1¾ cups soup
Calories: 158, **Calories from Fat:** 15%, **Total Fat:** 3g,
Saturated Fat: <1g, **Cholesterol:** 68mg, **Sodium:** 304mg,
Carbohydrate: 7g, **Fiber:** 2g, **Protein:** 26g

Dietary Exchanges: 1½ Vegetable, 2½ Meat

Diner Egg Salad Sandwiches

6 eggs
2 tablespoons fat-free mayonnaise
1½ tablespoons sweet pickle relish
½ cup finely chopped celery
⅛ teaspoon salt
Black pepper (optional)
8 slices whole-grain bread

1. Place eggs in medium saucepan; add enough cold water to cover. Bring to a boil over high heat. Immediately reduce heat; simmer 10 minutes. Drain and peel eggs under cold running water.

2. Cut eggs in half. Discard four yolk halves or reserve for another use. Place eight remaining egg yolk halves in medium bowl; add mayonnaise and pickle relish. Mash with fork until well blended and creamy. Chop egg whites; add to yolk mixture with celery and salt. Stir until well blended. Season to taste with pepper, if desired.

3. Spread ½ cup egg salad on each of four bread slices; top with remaining bread slices. *Makes 4 servings*

Nutrients per Serving: 1 sandwich
Calories: 253, **Calories from Fat:** 34%, **Total Fat:** 10g,
Saturated Fat: 3g, **Cholesterol:** 318mg, **Sodium:** 551mg,
Carbohydrate: 28g, **Fiber:** 4g, **Protein:** 15g

Dietary Exchanges: 2 Starch, 1½ Meat, 1 Fat

Southwestern Sloppy Joes

1 pound 95% lean ground beef
1 cup chopped onion
¼ cup chopped celery
¼ cup water
1 can (10 ounces) diced tomatoes with green chiles
1 can (8 ounces) no-salt-added tomato sauce
4 teaspoons brown sugar
½ teaspoon ground cumin
¼ teaspoon salt
9 whole wheat hamburger buns

1. Heat large nonstick skillet over high heat. Add beef, onion, celery and water; reduce heat to medium-high. Cook 6 to 8 minutes, stirring to break up meat. Drain fat.

2. Stir in tomatoes, tomato sauce, brown sugar, cumin and salt; bring to a boil over high heat. Reduce heat; simmer 20 minutes or until mixture thickens.

3. To serve, spoon ⅓ cup meat mixture onto each bun.

Makes 9 servings

Nutrients per Serving: 1 sandwich
Calories: 190, **Calories from Fat:** 19%, **Total Fat:** 4g,
Saturated Fat: 1g, **Cholesterol:** 15mg, **Sodium:** 413mg,
Carbohydrate: 26g, **Fiber:** 1g, **Protein:** 13g

Dietary Exchanges: 1 Vegetable, 1½ Starch, 1 Meat

Now you can have your beef and heart health, too—just be sure the beef is lean. Beef is rich in nutrients so it packs a healthy dose of vitamins and minerals including iron, zinc and B vitamins.

Thai Chicken Broccoli Salad

4 ounces uncooked linguine
½ pound boneless skinless chicken breasts, cut into
    bite-size pieces
2 cups broccoli florets
2 tablespoons cold water
⅔ cup chopped red bell pepper
6 green onions, sliced diagonally into 1-inch pieces
¼ cup reduced-fat creamy peanut butter
2 tablespoons hot water
2 tablespoons reduced-sodium soy sauce
2 teaspoons dark sesame oil
½ teaspoon red pepper flakes
⅛ teaspoon garlic powder
¼ cup unsalted peanuts, chopped

1. Cook pasta according to package directions, omitting salt. Drain; set aside.

2. Spray large nonstick skillet with nonstick cooking spray; heat over medium-high heat. Add chicken; cook and stir 5 minutes or until chicken is cooked through. Transfer to large bowl; set aside.

3. Add broccoli and cold water to skillet. Cook, covered, 2 minutes over medium-high heat. Uncover; cook and stir 2 minutes or until broccoli is crisp-tender. Add broccoli, pasta, bell pepper and green onions to chicken in bowl.

4. Whisk peanut butter, hot water, soy sauce, oil, red pepper flakes and garlic powder in small bowl until well blended. Drizzle over salad; toss to coat. Top with peanuts before serving.

Makes 4 servings

Nutrients per Serving: about 1 cup salad
Calories: 275, **Calories from Fat:** 29%, **Total Fat:** 9g,
Saturated Fat: 2g, **Cholesterol:** 29mg, **Sodium:** 314mg,
Carbohydrate: 29g, **Fiber:** 4g, **Protein:** 20g

Dietary Exchanges: 1 Vegetable, 1½ Starch, 2 Meat, ½ Fat

Crustless Ham and Asparagus Quiche

2 cups sliced asparagus (½-inch pieces)
1 red bell pepper, cut into ¼-inch dice
1 tablespoon water
1 cup low-fat (1%) milk
2 tablespoons all-purpose flour
4 egg whites
1 egg
1 cup chopped cooked deli ham, cut into ¼-inch dice
2 tablespoons chopped fresh tarragon or basil
½ teaspoon salt (optional)
¼ teaspoon black pepper
½ cup finely shredded Swiss cheese

1. Preheat oven to 350°F. Combine asparagus, bell pepper and water in medium microwavable bowl. Cover with waxed paper; microwave on HIGH 2 minutes or until vegetables are crisp-tender. Drain.

2. Whisk milk and flour in large bowl until well blended. Whisk in egg whites and egg until well blended. Stir in vegetables, ham, tarragon, salt, if desired, and black pepper. Pour into 9-inch pie plate.

3. Bake 35 minutes. Sprinkle cheese over quiche; bake 5 minutes or until center is set and cheese is melted. Let stand 5 minutes before serving.   *Makes 6 servings*

Nutrients per Serving: 1 piece (⅙ of total recipe)
Calories: 138, **Calories from Fat:** 38%, **Total Fat:** 6g,
Saturated Fat: 3g, **Cholesterol:** 25mg, **Sodium:** 439mg,
Carbohydrate: 8g, **Fiber:** 1g, **Protein:** 13g

Dietary Exchanges: 1½ Vegetable, 1½ Meat, ½ Fat

Tomato-Herb Soup

1 can (about 14 ounces) no-salt-added diced tomatoes
1 can (about 14 ounces) reduced-sodium chicken or vegetable broth
½ cup water
1 bag (8 ounces) frozen bell pepper strips
1 cup frozen green beans
1 tablespoon ketchup
1 to 2 teaspoons dried oregano
1 teaspoon dried basil
⅛ teaspoon red pepper flakes (optional)
1 tablespoon olive oil
½ teaspoon salt (optional)

1. Combine tomatoes, broth, water, bell peppers, green beans, ketchup, oregano, basil and red pepper flakes, if desired, in large saucepan. Bring to a boil over high heat. Reduce heat to low. Cover and simmer 20 minutes or until beans are tender and mixture thickens slightly.

2. Remove from heat. Stir in oil and salt, if desired. Let stand 5 minutes before serving.   *Makes 4 servings*

Nutrients per Serving: 1 cup
Calories: 94, **Calories from Fat:** 28%, **Total Fat:** 3g,
Saturated Fat: <1g, **Cholesterol:** 0mg, **Sodium:** 327mg,
Carbohydrate: 14g, **Fiber:** 4g, **Protein:** 3g

Dietary Exchanges: 1 Starch, ½ Fat

tip

Substitute chopped fresh bell peppers for the frozen bell pepper strips.

Chicken and Vegetable Wraps

SAUCE
- 2 tablespoons raspberry or strawberry fruit spread
- 2 tablespoons reduced-sodium soy sauce
- ⅛ teaspoon red pepper flakes

FILLING
- 2 teaspoons canola oil
- 3 cups thinly sliced purple cabbage
- 6 ounces asparagus spears, trimmed and cut into ½-inch pieces (about 1½ cups)
- ½ cup thinly sliced carrots
- 1 cup chopped green onions (about 8 green onions)
- 4 (6-inch) low-carb flour tortillas, warmed
- ¼ cup chopped cilantro
- ¼ cup peanuts, toasted and chopped
- 1 cup diced cooked chicken breast

1. Place fruit spread in small microwavable bowl; microwave on HIGH 15 seconds or until slightly melted. Stir in soy sauce and red pepper flakes; set aside.

2. Heat oil in large nonstick skillet over medium-high heat. Add cabbage, asparagus and carrots; cook and stir 2 minutes. Add onions; cook and stir 2 to 3 minutes or until cabbage is slightly wilted.

3. Spoon about 1 cup cabbage mixture onto each tortilla. Top each with 1 tablespoon sauce, 1 tablespoon cilantro, 1 tablespoon peanuts and ¼ cup chicken. Fold sides up over filling to create wrap.   *Makes 4 servings*

Nutrients per Serving: 1 wrap
Calories: 227, **Calories from Fat:** 36%, **Total Fat:** 9g, **Saturated Fat:** 1g, **Cholesterol:** 27mg, **Sodium:** 510mg, **Carbohydrate:** 27g, **Fiber:** 11g, **Protein:** 21g

Dietary Exchanges: 2 Vegetable, 1 Starch, 2 Meat, 1 Fat

Zucchini Cakes

3 teaspoons reduced-fat margarine, divided
2 tablespoons finely chopped red onion
1 medium zucchini, shredded
½ medium baking potato, peeled and shredded
¼ cup cholesterol-free egg substitute
4½ teaspoons plain dry bread crumbs
1 teaspoon chopped fresh dill
Pinch white pepper
Red onion rings (optional)

1. Melt 1½ teaspoons margarine in large nonstick skillet over medium heat. Add onion; cook and stir 5 minutes or until tender.

2. Combine onion, zucchini, potato, egg substitute, bread crumbs, dill and pepper in medium bowl; mix gently.

3. Melt remaining 1½ teaspoons margarine in large nonstick skillet over medium heat. Drop ¼ cupfuls of zucchini mixture into skillet and flatten with spatula. Cook 10 minutes or until golden brown, turning once. Garnish with onion rings, if desired.

Makes 2 servings

Nutrients per Serving: 2 zucchini cakes
Calories: 111, **Calories from Fat:** 24%, **Total Fat:** 3g,
Saturated Fat: 1g, **Cholesterol:** 0mg, **Sodium:** 123mg,
Carbohydrate: 17g, **Fiber:** 1g, **Protein:** 5g

Dietary Exchanges: ½ Vegetable, 1 Starch, ½ Fat

Layered Mexican Salad

1 package (10 ounces) shredded lettuce
½ cup chopped green onions
½ cup fat-free sour cream
⅓ cup picante sauce
1 medium lime, halved
1 teaspoon sugar
½ teaspoon ground cumin
1 medium avocado, peeled, seeded and chopped
¾ cup (3 ounces) shredded reduced-fat sharp
    Cheddar cheese
2 ounces baked tortilla chips, coarsely crumbled

1. Spread lettuce in 13×9-inch baking dish. Top evenly with green onions.

2. Combine sour cream, picante sauce, juice from one lime half, sugar and cumin; mix well. Spoon evenly over green onions. Top evenly with avocado. Squeeze remaining lime half evenly over avocado. Top evenly with cheese.

3. Cover with plastic wrap and refrigerate until ready to serve. (May be prepared 8 hours in advance, if desired.) Sprinkle with crumbled tortilla chips before serving.   *Makes 8 servings*

Nutrients per Serving: 1 cup
Calories: 118, **Calories from Fat:** 38%, **Total Fat:** 5g,
Saturated Fat: 2g, **Cholesterol:** 10mg, **Sodium:** 208mg,
Carbohydrate: 13g, **Fiber:** 3g, **Protein:** 5g

Dietary Exchanges: 1 Starch, 1 Fat

Spinach and Sausage Pizza

2 ready-made whole wheat pizza crusts (5 ounces each)
1 link (3 ounces) smoked turkey sausage, thinly sliced
½ cup fat-free ricotta cheese
2 tablespoons grated Parmesan cheese
1 clove garlic, crushed
½ teaspoon Italian seasoning
2 cups baby spinach leaves, coarsely chopped
2 plum tomatoes, thinly sliced
½ cup (2 ounces) shredded reduced-fat mozzarella cheese

1. Preheat oven to 450°F. Place pizza crusts on baking sheet; set aside. Spray small nonstick skillet with nonstick cooking spray; heat over medium heat. Add sausage; cook until browned.

2. Combine ricotta cheese, Parmesan cheese, garlic and Italian seasoning in small bowl. Spread in thin layer over pizza crusts to within ½ inch of edge. Layer sausage evenly over cheese. Top with spinach, tomatoes and mozzarella cheese.

3. Bake 12 to 15 minutes or until cheese is melted and golden brown and edges are crisp.   *Makes 6 servings*

Nutrients per Serving: 2 slices
Calories: 210, **Calories from Fat:** 26%, **Total Fat:** 6g,
Saturated Fat: 3g, **Cholesterol:** 20mg, **Sodium:** 525mg,
Carbohydrate: 28g, **Fiber:** 5g, **Protein:** 12g

Dietary Exchanges: 2 Starch, 1 Meat, ½ Fat

Spicy Black Bean Soup

2 teaspoons olive oil
1 small onion, chopped
1 cup thinly sliced carrots
2 jalapeño peppers,* seeded and minced
2 cloves garlic, minced
1 can (about 15 ounces) no-salt-added black beans,
    undrained
1 can (about 14 ounces) vegetable or chicken broth
¼ cup reduced-fat sour cream
¼ cup chopped fresh cilantro
4 lime wedges (optional)

*Jalapeño peppers can sting and irritate the skin, so wear rubber gloves when handling peppers and do not touch your eyes.

1. Heat oil in large saucepan over medium heat. Add onion, carrots, jalapeños and garlic; cook and stir 5 minutes.

2. Add beans and broth; bring to a boil. Reduce heat to low; cover and simmer 15 to 20 minutes or until vegetables are very tender. If desired, process soup in a food processor or blender until smooth, or use hand-held immersion blender.

3. Ladle soup into bowls; top with sour cream and cilantro. Serve with lime wedges, if desired.   *Makes 4 servings*

Nutrients per Serving: 1 cup
Calories: 163, **Calories from Fat:** 21%, **Total Fat:** 4g,
Saturated Fat: 1g, **Cholesterol:** 5mg, **Sodium:** 245mg,
Carbohydrate: 25g, **Fiber:** 7g, **Protein:** 8g

Dietary Exchanges: 1½ Starch, 1 Meat

Bulgur, Tuna, Tomato and Avocado Salad

⅔ cup water
⅓ cup uncooked bulgur
1 cup halved grape tomatoes
1 can (6 ounces) tuna packed in water, drained and flaked
¼ cup finely chopped red onion
1 large stalk celery, trimmed and thinly sliced
¼ cup finely chopped avocado
1 tablespoon minced fresh Italian parsley
1 to 2 tablespoons lemon juice
4 teaspoons chicken broth
1 teaspoon olive oil
⅛ teaspoon black pepper

1. Bring water to a boil in small saucepan. Stir in bulgur. Reduce heat to low; cover and simmer 8 minutes or until bulgur swells and has absorbed most of the water. Remove from heat; cover and let stand 10 minutes.

2. Meanwhile, combine tomatoes, tuna, onion and celery in large bowl. Stir in bulgur, avocado and parsley.

3. Whisk lemon juice, broth, oil and pepper in small bowl until well blended. Pour over salad; toss gently to coat. Cover and refrigerate 2 hours before serving.   *Makes 3 servings*

Nutrients per Serving: 1 cup
Calories: 166, **Calories from Fat:** 21%, **Total Fat:** 4g,
Saturated Fat: 1g, **Cholesterol:** 17mg, **Sodium:** 221mg,
Carbohydrate: 17g, **Fiber:** 4g, **Protein:** 17g

Dietary Exchanges: 1 Starch, 1 Meat

tip

Bulgur wheat is wheat that has been steamed, dried and crushed. It is in the rice and dried beans or natural foods aisle of the supermarket.

Spicy Mexican Frittata

1 jalapeño pepper*
1 clove garlic
1 medium tomato, peeled, quartered and seeded
½ teaspoon chili powder
½ cup chopped onion
1 cup frozen corn
6 egg whites
2 eggs
¼ cup fat-free (skim) milk
¼ teaspoon salt
¼ teaspoon black pepper
¼ cup (1 ounce) shredded part-skim farmer or
    mozzarella cheese

1. Place jalapeño pepper and garlic in food processor or blender; process until finely chopped. Add tomato and chili powder; process until tomato is almost smooth.

2. Spray large nonstick skillet with nonstick cooking spray; heat over medium heat. Add onion; cook and stir until tender. Stir in tomato mixture and corn; cook and stir 3 to 4 minutes or until liquid is almost evaporated.

3. Combine egg whites, eggs, milk, salt and black pepper in medium bowl. Add egg mixture to skillet. Cook without stirring 2 minutes or until eggs begin to set. Run large spoon around edge of skillet, lifting eggs for even cooking. Remove skillet from heat when eggs are almost set but surface is still moist.

4. Sprinkle with cheese. Cover and let stand 3 to 4 minutes or until surface is set and cheese is melted   *Makes 4 servings*

Nutrients per Serving: 1 frittata wedge (¼ of total recipe)
Calories: 129, **Calories from Fat:** 22%, **Total Fat:** 3g,
Saturated Fat: 1g, **Cholesterol:** 108mg, **Sodium:** 371mg,
Carbohydrate: 14g, **Fiber:** 2g, **Protein:** 12g

Dietary Exchanges: 1 Vegetable, ½ Starch, 1 Meat

Garlic Bread and Salmon Salad

2 slices day-old light whole wheat bread
1 clove garlic, cut in half
1 can (7½ ounces) salmon, drained and flaked
1 cup cherry or grape tomatoes, halved
½ cup chopped green onions
5 teaspoons white wine vinegar
1 tablespoon tomato juice
1 teaspoon olive oil
¼ teaspoon salt
¼ teaspoon pepper
2 tablespoons chopped fresh basil

1. Place rack 3 to 4 inches from heat source; preheat broiler. Rub one side of each bread slice with garlic; discard garlic. Place bread, garlic side up, on broiler rack. Broil 20 to 30 seconds or until lightly browned; watch carefully to avoid burning. When cool enough to handle, cut bread into 1-inch pieces.

2. Combine salmon, tomatoes and green onions in large bowl. Whisk vinegar, tomato juice, oil, salt and pepper in small bowl until well blended. Pour over salmon mixture. Add garlic bread cubes; toss gently. Sprinkle with basil. *Makes 4 servings*

Nutrients per Serving: 1 cup salad
Calories: 123, **Calories from Fat:** 29%, **Total Fat:** 4g,
Saturated Fat: 1g, **Cholesterol:** 44mg, **Sodium:** 430mg,
Carbohydrate: 8g, **Fiber:** 2g, **Protein:** 15g

Dietary Exchanges: ½ Starch, 2 Meat